Life, Unassembled

The Chapters In Between

A Soft Power Series Book

Elaine Hayoz

Copyright © 2026 by Elaine Hayoz

All rights reserved.

First paperback edition.

Published by Lightfield Press
An imprint of ESH Consulting LLC

Paperback ISBN: 978-1-972932-05-6

No part of this book may be reproduced, distributed, or transmitted in any form or by any means, including electronic or mechanical methods, including photocopying, recording, or any information storage and retrieval system, without prior written permission of the publisher, except in the case of brief quotations embodied in reviews and certain other noncommercial uses permitted by copyright law.

This book is a work of nonfiction based on the author's personal experience and reflection. Any resemblance to other persons, living or dead, beyond the author's own lived experience, is coincidental.

This book is not intended as medical, psychological, legal, or professional advice. It is not a substitute for professional care. Readers are encouraged to use their own discernment and seek appropriate professional support when needed.

elainehayoz.com

For you

A Note to the Reader

This book is not meant to be rushed.

You may find yourself reading a page
And then pausing. Or returning to a chapter more than once. Or noticing how your body feels as much as what the words say.

This is intentional.

You don't need to read this book in order.
You don't need to understand everything at once.
You can open it where you are and let
it meet you there.

Take what resonates.
Leave what doesn't.

Let ease set the pace.

Foreword

I have found myself many times in between chapters.

Over the past several years, I found myself looking at a map that no longer fit the life I was living.

A long marriage ended.
Work fell away.
My mother passed away.
My children grew into their own lives.

My north star shifted and the familiar directions I once trusted no longer pointed forward.

In the quiet that followed, I realized I no longer knew what brought me joy. I had given so much of myself to family, to marriage, and work that I was no longer sure who I was apart from them.

Some days I felt steady.
Other days I felt like a shell of a person I used to be.

Rebuilding did not begin with clarity.
It began with small questions.
What feels true?
What feels alive?

What followed was not quick or tidy.
There was an excavation.
An examination.
A re-evaluation of who I thought I was,
who I was becoming,
and what truly mattered.

Much of that time was spent in pause. Not knowing where I was headed, only knowing that the old path no longer showed me where I was going or who I was anymore.

I learned that alignment does not come from forcing a new direction, but from staying present long enough to hear what remains true.

What I found in that space was not failure.
I found resilience in the pause, and the comfort in the place between chapters.

I also found that something new does not announce itself all at once; it begins quietly, long before it can be named.

This book was written from there.

It is not a guide for fixing your life or finding answers quickly. It is an offering of companionship. A reminder that these in-between places are real, meaningful, and shared.

If you are holding this book because something in your life has shifted, unraveled, or gone quiet, I hope this brings you one simple knowing:

You are not alone with this.

Chapter 1
The Chapters In Between

There are times when the familiar
markers fall away.

Sometimes abruptly.
Sometimes in ways that leave the ground
beneath you feeling unstable, as though
what once held you no longer does.

Sometimes quietly.
Not all at once, and not dramatically.
More like a slow realization that the map
you've been following no longer speaks to who
you are, or where you are now.

And sometimes, there is a gentle sense of relief.
Not because everything is clear, but because an
opening is beginning to make itself felt.

Not an answer.
Not a plan.
Just the quiet recognition that something
new may now be allowed to begin.

You may notice it in small ways:
a pause before responding,
a longer look out the window,
a subtle awareness that the version of you
who carried the old map is no longer
the one standing here.

Not lost.
Just between directions.

This space can feel unfamiliar at first.
The old reference points no longer guide you,
and the next ones haven't appeared yet.

You may find yourself
reaching for certainty,
checking your phone,
replaying conversations,
wondering if you missed something.

It's easy to think something has gone wrong.
That you should already know what comes next.

This place is not a mistake.
It's a pause.

It is a chapter in your life that doesn't
hurry toward urgency.
It doesn't require answers or action.

It simply asks that you remain present.

This book isn't here to tell you what to do next.

It's here to stay with you in this space while the
way forward is still unfolding.

There is nowhere to go,
nothing to do,
just be.

You don't need to rush out of this place
to be worthy of peace.

Something steady remains,
even when direction grows quiet.

You can move through this moment
in your life without forcing what comes next.

This book stays with you here.

Chapter 2
When the Map Grows Quiet

There is a moment when direction softens.
Not because you've failed to follow it,
but because it no longer applies to where you are.

What once guided you
stops offering clear instruction.
The familiar signs fade.
The certainty you relied on becomes quiet.

You may find yourself refreshing your inbox,
checking for something new,
as though clarity might arrive in bold letters.

This can feel unsettling.

The instinct is often to search for a replacement.
A new plan, a new goal, a new answer.
Something to restore the feeling of movement.

A quiet map is not a broken one.

Sometimes
it simply means
you are being asked to listen differently.

This is not a test of your resolve.
It is not a demand for immediate clarity.
It is an invitation to notice where you are
without trying to define where you are going.

When the map grows quiet,
nothing essential has been taken from you.
The way forward has not disappeared.
It is simply not speaking yet.

Silence
is
not
absence.

It is a different kind of guidance.

You are allowed to pause here
without interpreting the quiet as loss.

Chapter 3
This Place Is Not a Mistake

It's easy to believe that if you had chosen differently, you wouldn't be here.

That if you had known more, moved faster, or listened sooner, this place would not exist.

You may find yourself running through quiet "what if" scenarios.
Replaying small moments, adjusting your tone, your timing, your courage — as though history were still open for revision.

This place is not evidence of error.
It is not a detour you need to explain away.
It is not a consequence you need to justify.

It is part of your journey.

Being here doesn't mean you misread the signs.
It means something in your life shifted before the next direction was ready to appear.

This place does not require self-correction.

It does not ask you to rewrite the past.
It simply allows you to stand where you are without assigning meaning too quickly.

Nothing needs to be fixed for this place to be valid.

You are not behind.
You are not failing.
You are here.

And
here
is
allowed.

Chapter 4
Not Lost. Just Here.

When direction falls away,
the word lost often appears.

Lost implies
you were meant to be somewhere else.

This place
asks for a different understanding.

You are not lost.
You are present in a space
that has not yet named itself.

There is a difference between
disorientation and absence.

You may find yourself
reaching for directions —
opening a map,
checking it twice,
as though clarity might load
more quickly the second time.

You may ask someone
what they think you should do,
then sense,
quietly,
that the guidance doesn't quite fit.

That is not failure.
It is human.

You may not know where you are going,
yet something steady holds.

This place can hold you
without demanding movement.

You don't have to define it.
You don't have to explain it to anyone.
You don't even have to like it yet.

You only need to know that being here
does not mean you've failed to arrive.

It means you have arrived
somewhere
quieter than expected.

And that is enough.

Resting Place

You can stop here.

Let the page remain open
for a moment longer.

Nothing is required.
There is nowhere else
you need to be.

If thoughts are circling,
they can circle.
If the breath feels uneven,
it will settle in its own time.

This moment does not need
to become anything.

It does not need to be solved
before you step away.

The chair beneath you.

The quiet in the room.
Even a small corner of it.
That is enough.

You are not carrying this alone.
For now,
rest.

Chapter 5
Laying It Down

There is a moment when carrying
becomes heavier than releasing.

Not because you've reached the end of
your strength — but because something
deeper knows this weight was never
meant to be held this way.

You may have been carrying it carefully.
Responsibly.
Quietly.
Doing what needed to be done.
Showing up.
Staying upright.

Holding everything together
long after it began to loosen.

Perhaps you believed it was your job
to anticipate every outcome.
To smooth every edge.
To make sure nothing else fell apart.

You may have called it strength.
Or responsibility.
Or simply being the reliable one.

And maybe it was.
But somewhere along the way,
control began to feel like survival.

And survival is a heavy thing to carry.

Sometimes the weight you are carrying
is not the circumstance itself,
but the constant effort to avoid feeling it.

Keeping busy.
Keeping cheerful.
Keeping distracted.

Distraction can look like resilience.

Until you are tired.

Until one day, the effort itself begins
to ask a different question:

What if you didn't have to hold this right now?

Laying it down doesn't mean you're done
with it forever. It doesn't mean you've given up.

It doesn't mean you've failed some invisible test.

It means you are allowing yourself a pause
from carrying what has become too heavy
to lift alone.

Sometimes laying it down happens in words.
Sometimes it happens in silence.

Sometimes it happens without language at all,
just a moment where the body stops bracing and
something inside exhales.

You may not know where to place
what you're holding.
You may quietly wonder
if anything is there to receive it.

And yet, when you loosen your grip,
something steadies.

Not loudly.
Not dramatically.
Just enough to let you breathe again.

You only know that you are tired.
And that knowing is enough.

Laying it down is not a decision you force.
It's a response to your exhale.

A quiet recognition
that you are not required
to solve everything before you rest.

You can set it down gently.

You don't need to drop it in urgency or
collapse in despair from the release.

There is no rush here.

Nothing essential is lost when you loosen
your hold.

What matters remains.
What isn't ready to be carried can wait.

And sometimes,
when you stop gripping so tightly,
you discover you were never the
only one holding it.

You are allowed to rest in this place
without knowing what comes next.

You are allowed to be supported
without understanding how.

Laying it down is not the end of your strength.
It is the beginning of relief.

And relief, when it comes softly,
has a way of making room
for what comes after.

For now, it is enough
to stop holding.

You can lay it down,
just for this moment.

Chapter 6

What Holds When You Stop Holding

Once the grip softens,
something unexpected becomes visible.

Not dramatically.
Not in a way that announces itself.

More like a subtle realization that nothing has fallen apart in the way you feared it might.

You are still here.
Still breathing.
Still aware.
Still steady enough.

After you stop holding
everything so tightly,
there is often a moment of surprise.

Something quieter begins to register.
There is steadiness that was present even
while you were striving.

The sky above you.
The solid ground beneath your feet.
The air that fills your lungs.
The soft breeze that touches your skin.

There is a support that does not depend on your effort.

It does not rush you.
It does not ask you to prove yourself first.
It does not withhold itself until you have figured everything out.

It remains.

You may have spent a long time searching
for clearer instructions — waiting for certainty
to arrive in an unmistakable form.
A sign with brighter lighting, bigger font.
A message that removes all doubt.

However, what holds you, does not shout.

It does not compete with noise.
It does not perform.
It simply stays.

And in the staying, you begin to notice
something else: you were never carrying this alone
in the way you thought you were.

Not everything depended on your strength.
Not every outcome required your management.
Not every silence meant abandonment.

There is a presence here.

Quiet.

Unforced.

Steady.

You don't have to name it.
You don't have to define it.
You don't even have to fully believe in it yet.

You only have to notice
that when you soften,
something steadies you.

What holds you
does not require you to be perfect.

It does not require you
to have the right words,
the right plan,
or the right timing.

It remains
whether you are certain
or unsure.

Nothing here demands movement.

Just presence.

And as you stay, you may begin to sense
that this quiet support has been here longer
than you realized.

Not demanding.
Not dramatic.

Just enough.

You are still here.

And
you
are
held.

Chapter 7
Staying Without Answers

There is a particular discomfort
that comes with not knowing what comes next.

Not the kind that asks to be solved.
The kind that simply waits.

We are taught, often without realizing it,
that not knowing is an issue.
That uncertainty means something
is unfinished. Or wrong.

When answers don't arrive quickly,
the instinct is to search harder.
To decide something. Anything.
Just to regain a sense of movement.

You may find yourself scanning for signs
you've missed. As though clearer instructions
were posted somewhere and you simply
overlooked them.

As though next time the universe might
put a large blinking arrow pointing to the sign,
to the path forward.

There are places where answers do not yet belong.

This is one of them.

Staying without answers doesn't mean you've
stopped caring.

It means you are honoring the timing
of what hasn't yet revealed itself.

There is a difference between

being stuck

and being still.

Stillness does not demand resolution.
It allows what is unfinished
to remain unfinished
without turning it into failure.

You may notice a quiet urge
to move past this place.

To gather clarity before resting.
To make a plan so you can relax.

There may be evenings
when you sit in your car

longer than necessary,

hands resting on the steering wheel,
watching the light shift
on the windshield.

You tell yourself
you're just finishing a song.

Really,
you're gathering yourself, for the next small thing.

You may draft a text message
and rewrite it three times,
wondering which version of you is responding:
the steady one,
the hopeful one,
or the one still figuring it out.

You may reach for your phone
without remembering the
moment you picked it up.
Scroll past other people's lives
as though one of them
might contain
a clue
about yours.

You may start another episode.
Another podcast.
Let voices fill the room
to keep your thoughts at bay.

You may pour a second glass
not because you are celebrating,
but because you would rather blur than sit.

You may snack without hunger.

Stay busy without direction.
Answer messages immediately so you
don't have to feel the pause.

None of this means something is wrong with you.

It makes you human.

When quiet feels uncertain,
we look for something
that feels like movement.

This is not confusion.

It is recalibration.

Sometimes rest comes first.
Sometimes peace arrives
before understanding does.

Staying here
is not passive.

It is an act of trust,
even if you don't yet know what you're trusting.

You are choosing not to force an answer
before it knows how to speak.

You are choosing to live

at the speed of trust

rather than the speed of fear.

Some might call this surrender.
Not the kind that defeats you.
The kind that frees you.
The kind that opens rather than collapses.

Trust does not rush.
It does not panic when the path is unclear.

It allows what is forming
to take its time
becoming visible.

This place asks for very little.

Only that you stay present
to what is here now.

The breath.
The stillness.
The quiet support.

You do not have to like this space
to let it be what it is.

You do not have to name it
or explain it
or make meaning of it yet.

You can remain without answers
and still be supported.

Nothing essential is forgotten
when clarity takes its time.

What is meant to come
will arrive in its own way,
in its own time.

For now, it is enough
to rest.

Chapter 8
Being Met Here

There are moments
when something shifts —
not because circumstances change,
but because you realize
you are not alone here.

It doesn't arrive loudly.
There is no announcement.
No dramatic turning point.

It feels more like warmth than certainty.
More like presence than direction.

You may not be able to name when it began.
Only that something feels steadier than before.
As though the room has softened.
As though the air has changed.

Being met here doesn't mean everything makes sense now. It doesn't mean answers have arrived or decisions have been made.

It means
you are not carrying this moment by yourself.

Support often arrives quietly, without instruction, without explanation, without an outline.

It meets you where you are,
not where you think you should be.

It does not ask you to improve first.
It does not require you to be stronger,
clearer, or more certain.

It simply stays.

You don't have to reach for it.
You don't have to perform belief.
You don't have to be ready.
It is already here.

You may notice it in the way your breath settles
before you are even conscious of it.

In the way your shoulders drop
when no one is asking anything from you.

In the quiet sense that you are allowed to be
exactly as you are in this moment.

Being met here
does not mean the path is revealed.

It means you are accompanied
while it unfolds.

And sometimes,
that
is
enough.

Chapter 9
Stillness Is Not Empty

Stillness is often misunderstood.
It's mistaken for waiting.
For absence.
For a lack of progress.

For the space where something should be happening, but isn't.

When life grows quiet,
the instinct is to fill the space.
To reorganize a closet,
to research something new,
to refresh your social media
as though clarity might arrive as a notification.

To make sure you are not falling behind in a race no one officially announced.

Sometimes stillness
feels like exposure.
Like standing in a room without distractions
and realizing you are alone with yourself.

We are not always taught how to be with the quiet.

So, we create noise.

A show playing in the background.

Music loud enough to interrupt a thought.

Another episode.
Another snack.
Another scroll.

We plan a future that is not yet asking
to be planned.

Motion can feel safer than presence.

But stillness is not emptiness.
It is unfamiliarity.

We often fill silence
before we learn
how to sit inside it.

Not because we are broken.
Because stillness can feel unfamiliar
before it feels safe.

Stillness is not a gap in the story.
It may be where the story gathers itself.

It may be that something is taking shape
beneath the surface.

Not dramatically.

Not in ways you can measure.

More like roots
extending underground
before anything appears
above ground.

Roots do not announce themselves.
They do not send updates.
They do not ask for applause.

Sometimes, the most beautiful plants
emerge from the rockiest of soils.

Stillness does not look productive.
There are no visible milestones.
No gold stars.
No confirmation email telling you
you are exactly where you should be.

And yet, something may be forming.

You may not feel inspired.
You may not feel certain.
You may not even feel peaceful.

Some days stillness feels like rest.
Other days it feels
suspiciously
like
nothing.

Formation does not require emotion.
It requires space.

Stillness creates that space.

It allows what is real
to rise
without being forced.

You are not disappearing here.
You may simply be becoming
less distracted.

You are not paused in life.
You may be more
rooted than you realize.

What needs to surface
will surface.

What needs to loosen
will loosen.

What needs to grow,
is already reaching quietly.

Stillness is not empty.
It may be gestation of something greater
than you can imagine.

Unseen movement.
Life gathering strength
before it asks to be lived out loud.

And you do not have to rush it.

Resting Place

Stay.
Not because nothing is happening,
but because something is.

You may not see it yet.
You may not feel it clearly.
Beneath the quiet,
something is gathering.

There is no need to rush it.
No need to name it.
Remain long enough to sense
that this pause is not empty.
It is forming.

The breath moves in.
The breath moves out.

Readiness does not announce itself.
It gathers quietly.

Rest here, not as escape,
but as quiet preparation.
There is nowhere else to go.
Nothing to force.

Only this moment, steady and alive.
Stay.

Chapter 10
When the Next Step Isn't Visible Yet

There comes a moment
when you realize the quiet has not ended,
and that it does not need to.

The path forward has not revealed itself.
You may still not know what comes next.
No clear direction has appeared.
No plan has assembled itself around you.

And yet,
something feels different.

The urgency has softened.
The pressure to decide
no longer grips as tightly.

Not because answers have arrived.
Because you are no longer demanding
that they hurry.

Not every step appears before it is needed.
Some only become visible
once you stop straining
to see beyond where you stand.

We are often taught to move as soon
as uncertainty appears.
To choose quickly.

To make something happen, anything to happen,
as if movement can force a positive outcome.

There are places where movement
does not respond to force.

It responds to readiness.

When the next step isn't visible yet,
it does not mean you are standing still forever,
even thought it may feel like it.

It means the way forward is still forming.
Quietly, beneath the surface.

You are not behind.
You are not late.
You are tuning in.

Listening does not look like anticipation.
It looks like remaining open
without demanding clarity
before it has taken shape.

It does not require a mission statement,
or a color-coded five-year plan drafted
in a surge of late-night determination.

It asks for something quieter.

You may begin to notice
small signals instead of instructions.

A sense of ease

where there was tension before.

A gentle pull
rather than a push.

These are not decisions.
They are invitations.

You do not need to act on
them immediately.
You can let them gather.
Let them settle.

Trust is not urgency.

Trust is a willingness
to let what is forming
arrive softly.
It allows
the next step
to come toward you
rather than chasing it down.

For now,
it is enough to remain where you are
and allow what wants to move
to take its time to become visible.

The path does not disappear
just because you cannot see it.

It is not absent.

It is remembering.

And when it becomes clear,

you will recognize it,

not by pressure,

but by resonance.

Chapter 11
Listening for What Remains

When much has fallen away,
there is often a quiet fear
that nothing is left.

That the letting go went too far.
That the quiet took something with it.

What remains
is rarely loud.

It does not announce itself.
It does not demand recognition.

It waits.

Listening for what remains is different
from listening for what's next.

It is not about discovering something new.

It is about recognizing
what did not leave.

What stayed even when everything
else shifted.

What remains
often reveals itself
as something
simple.

A value that did not waver.
A boundary that was respected.
A tenderness that did not harden.
A way of being that still feels like home.

You may notice it in what continues to matter,
even now.

In what you protect without effort.
In what brings a quiet sense of ease
rather than excitement.

This kind of listening does not rush to define itself.

It does not require another vision board
or more manifestation mantras.

It unfolds in recognition.

What remains
is not always what you expected.

Sometimes it is smaller.
Sometimes it is softer.
Sometimes, it is grace.

Sometimes
it is simply the knowing that you still care.

And that matters.

You do not have to build your future
from it yet.

You do not have to extract meaning from it.

For now, it is enough to notice
that not everything was lost.
That not everything needs to be rebuilt.
That some things endured.

Listening for what remains
is an act of respect
for the part of you
that stayed present
when everything else was uncertain.

It is a way of allowing the next chapter
in your life to take shape around
what is real rather than what urgency invents.

What remains does not push you forward.

It stands with you.

And when movement comes,
it will rise
from what has stayed true.

Chapter 12
Carrying Peace Forward

Peace
does not always announce itself as calm.

Sometimes it shows up

as a little more space

inside the same circumstances.

A softer response.
A steadier breath.
A quieter return to yourself.

You may not have noticed it arriving.

It may have been forming slowly —
without a clear moment of change.

Carrying peace forward
does not mean leaving this place behind.

It means recognizing
that what steadied you here
is not dependent on stillness alone.

Peace shaped in quiet
does not disappear
when life begins to move again.

It knows how to remain

alongside uncertainty,
alongside questions,
alongside days that do not feel resolved.

You don't need to protect it.

You don't need to maintain it perfectly.

It has already learned how to stay.

You may notice it in how you pause
before responding.
You do not rush to fill the quiet
in the way you once did.

You have learned how to sit inside it.

Silence is no longer something to escape.
It has become a place you recognize.

You may notice
it in how you allow things to unfold
without resistance.

There was a time when quiet felt too exposed.

When you reached for noise before you knew why.
You do not reach as quickly now to fill it.

You do not rush to smooth it over anymore.

Not perfectly.
Not every time.

But often enough to trust yourself here.

You may even begin to welcome the quiet.

You are not leaving this place.
You are carrying it.

Movement does not require abandoning
what you found here.

It simply asks that you trust yourself
to move with it
and not away from it.

You may still not know everything.
You may still not see the entire path.
You are no longer divided against yourself.

And that changes everything.

The place that once felt like a pause
has become a foundation.

You are not stepping out
of the chapters in between.

You are stepping from them.

Grounded.
Aware.
Whole.

And when the way grows quiet again,
as it will — you will know what to do.

You will stay.
You will listen.

And when movement comes,
you
will
know
what
belongs.

About the Author

Elaine Hayoz is a writer whose work explores presence, pause, and the quiet strength found in life's in-between spaces. Shaped by seasons of change and reorientation, her writing reflects a deep trust in what forms when we remain with what is unfolding.

Through gentle language and spacious reflection, she offers steady companionship to those navigating transition, uncertainty,
and inner renewal.

Life, Unassembled is part of the *Soft Power Series*, a collection of reflective works exploring the space between what was and what comes next.

She lives in Colorado, where wide skies, flower-filled mountain meadows, and changing seasons echo the themes in her work.

www.ingramcontent.com/pod-product-compliance
Lightning Source LLC
LaVergne TN
LVHW011052110826
845149LV00015B/3462